I0477967

How Small Investors Can Get Started In Commercial Properties

A Beginner Guide to Buying Your First Commercial Property

BY

ERNIE BRAVEBOY

Get Your Free Copy of

How to be a Real Estate Millionaire

To Get Your Free Copy, Open the Link

https://ebraveboy_3ee2.gr8.com/

Introduction

I want to thank you and congratulate you for buying the book, *"How Small Investors Can Get Started In Commercial Properties: A Beginner Guide to Buying Your First Commercial Property"*.

This book has actionable information on how to get started in commercial real estate investing even if you are a complete beginner.

Forget residential real estate investing; commercial real estate is the way to go if you want the best bang for your buck. The only problem is that very few people dabble in commercial real estate investment, and therefore, there are fewer examples to consult and copy. In addition, when it comes to commercial real estate, reference material, both online and offline, tend to be a bit on the thin side, which is where this book comes in.

This guide shall take you through all the factors and elements you need to familiarize yourself with as you dip your toes into the commercial real estate investing pool for the first time. The sole aim of this guidebook is to ensure that when you turn the last page, you will have absorbed all the knowledge you need to buy your first commercial property without fear or uncertainty. Let's begin.

Thanks again for buying this book. I hope you enjoy it!

Table of Contents

Before we can discuss how to invest in commercial real estate, let me start by discussing whether investing in commercial real estate should be top on your priority list.

Should You Invest in Commercial Real Estate?

This section is going to look at whether the time is ripe for commercial real estate investment. It shall also delve into the questions you should ask yourself before you decide to "get in," as well as the decisions you need to make to ensure you survive longer than most.

The fact that you are reading this book is enough proof that you are determined to invest in commercial real estate—the search for knowledge is one of the beacons of someone determined.

Before you start implementing the knowledge this guidebook shall impart on you, begin by asking yourself a couple of important questions and by making a couple of vital decisions that this chapter shall outline and discuss.

Going over everything discussed in this chapter is very important because doing so will provide you with greater certainty that you are ready to invest in commercial property. It will also help you streamline the commercial property options you go for, which ultimately, will help you act with greater efficiency.

Ask Yourself These Questions First

Your answers to the following questions shall help you gain immense clarity of thought and action. Answer these questions as honestly and candidly as you can. Preferably, jot the answers in a notebook so that you give yourself to expound and personalize the answer as you deem fit:

Question 1: Do I have the necessary funds to invest in commercial property?

You may already know; nonetheless, we shall include it here for effect: commercial properties are always substantially more expensive than the likes of residential properties. As such, it is important to ensure that you have sufficient investment capital. If money is somewhat thin, this book will show you different strategies you can follow to fund your investment.

Question 2: Do I have any financial, trade, or business expertise that may prove valuable to my investment in commercial property?

This one is not a must-have. However, if you have some form of expertise that could be valuable to your investment strategy, such knowledge or expertise shall come in handy since it could steer you down a natural investment path. This will mean that right off the bat, you will have found a niche that works great for you, which will maximize your efficiency as well as the probability to succeed.

Here is an example: if you have spent the last 12 years in healthcare administration, you will be far better suited to investing in healthcare properties compared to a newbie who does not have that kind of experience.

The answers to these two questions will feature prominently in the decisions you make from hereon. Now that we are talking of the decisions you need to make, here are some:

Important Decisions to Make Regarding Your Commercial Property Investing

As you let the answers to the questions above marinate, consider the following decisions that you need to make

Decision 1: Decide how you want to invest in commercial property goes

What is it that you want to be? What roles do you want to play? Are you interested in being a landlord who is in ownership of commercial property or does it suit you better to be part of an investment group that purchases office buildings co-operatively?

When you work on your own, you will be shouldering all the risks and responsibilities that come with the package. However, as opposed to being part of an investment group, you will also be taking the whole cake home. Decide what you want to do with your investment ventures.

Decision 2: Decide how much money you can invest as well as how you will finance your investment

When it comes to funding your foray into commercial real estate investing, you can take several financing routes such as traditional loans, partnership investing, hard money loans, crowdfunding and so forth.

Section 8 will walk you through various financing routes. Give it a quick scan first before going back to it later and reading it more meticulously. Perhaps already have an idea on how you will finance your project. If that is the case, examine your current choices again and determine if they truly are the best for you.

Now that we have that in mind way, the other things we are going to discuss in this chapter are the pros and cons of commercial real estate investing. Delving into this will help you gauge where you stand, which will help you decide if investing in commercial real estate is the right thing for you:

The Pros and Cons of Commercial Real Estate Investing

It is always a great idea to understand what you are getting yourself into before you get into it. A great way to do this is to have a clear understanding of the pros and cons of the thing.

Commercial property tends to pay out in a big way, which is why most people who get into commercial property investment never back out. Still, like most investments, it also has a few cons you need to be familiar with and expect once you invest.

Here is an in-depth look at the pros and cons of investing in commercial property.

Pros of investing in commercial properties

The pros include:

Higher returns

Compared to residential properties, you will quickly discover that most of the time, commercial properties provide a higher ROI (return on investment). Take warehouses for example. The average rental yield sits at 8-10%. Compare this to the average rental yield for residential properties that sits at 3-6%.

Fewer "ongoing" expenses

Commercial tenants will typically cover rates such as the council, insurance, and water rates as well as body corporate

5

fees–if they are within the package. This will mean that as a commercial property owner, you will have fewer ongoing costs to foot. Compare this to most residential properties where you constantly have to foot some cost or other.

Longer leasing period

The average commercial property lease is between 3 and 10 years, which is a substantial amount of time. Compare this to residential property whose lease will—as is often the case—barely go past 12 months and even then, offers no guarantee of renewal.

The reasoning behind the differing lease term lengths is that commercial tenants tend to stay put for longer because they are most likely running a business. For a business to catch on, it needs some grounding. They also tend to stay put longer if they have invested capital to be able to acquire the property as well as improve it. For instance, it is common for a commercial tenant to spend $20,000 to fit out space and give it an improved, professional look. This will be enough to provide you with enough certainty and rental income security.

Prices are a lot more stable

Going by history, commercial properties tend to show far less fluctuation in value especially when compared to residential real estate. Property value bodies usually set the value of commercial property. This means you do not have to worry and haggle over the property you want to invest in, which is what you would do with residential real estate.

The presence of value-adding activity

As we said, it is common for a commercial tenant to get the wallet or purse open and spend their money to improve the look and feel of the space. These improvements on the layout and structure of the space will often greatly improve the value of the property.

Take the example of a new paint job and under-floor lighting: if the tenant does move away after a few years, it is unlikely that he or she shall carry the paint job or under-floor lighting structure as well. These improvements will further justify any higher pricing you may attach to space.

Such modifications are often very rare with residential property. In fact, the opposite is often true—the reason why it is smart to ask for a deposit amount beforehand is so that you are safe if the tenant decides to move away suddenly and you discover all sorts of damages to the premise.

The cons of investing in commercial properties

As far as commercial property cons go, we have to mention that the bulk of the greatest drawbacks stem from a lack of proper research and property knowledge, leasing your property to irresponsible tenants, and failing to inspect the property before investing in it.

Here are several cons to be watchful of:

A lack of ample property research:

We have said that property value bodies often decide the value of commercial property. This is good news for you

7

since it means fluctuations or absurd pricing will not be something you have to deal with often.

With this said, it is unwise to sit on your lily pad and assume safety; you need to do commercial property research and especially pay close attention to the market forces as you do so. Once you become the owner of a commercial property, do not make the mistake of being too strong-minded and refusing to deviate from the rental prices you have in mind.

Too often, a property owner will ignore the current market conditions and ask for bloated rental figures. This leads to a shortage of tenants. Ultimately, they have to place vacant for months on end, which will mean they lose a lot of revenue. Have your finger on the market pulse so that your rental rates make sense all around.

Vulnerability to economic factors

Unlike residential property that will have a steady stream of tenants regardless of the state of the economy, an economic dip, bloated interest rates, inflation, high rates of unemployment, and spells of poor business confidence (yes indeed, these spells do happen) such cases mean less demand for commercial properties. This will mean that quality tenants will be scarce. This leads us to...

Periods with no tenants

Commercial properties tend to pay out handsomely. However, unlike residential properties, they can be subject to long untenanted periods. Years could go by without tenants. During the interim, you will have to cover expenses until a tenant occupies the premises.

Upgrades tend to be costly

As is the case with all property investment kinds, upgrade costs will usually depend on the property type. However, renovating commercial properties such as an office or retail situation will be considerably more expensive than renovating a home.

The reason for this is that commercial property upgrades tend to demand a greater scope of work, for a larger area no less, and will include intensive renovation tasks such as asbestos removal, revamping of fire and safety installations, restructuring the space so that it better mirrors the tenant's business needs and changing the fit-out. Compare this to renovating a home whose bulk of tasks will be the inexpensive kind such as installing new appliances and giving the place a fresh paint job.

Now that you know this, let us go a step further and compare commercial real estate investing to residential property investing:

How Commercial Property Investing Stacks Up Against Investing In Residential Property

Beyond making side-by-side comparisons and educating you on the salient properties of both, this chapter will further educate you on what you can expect when you invest in commercial properties, with regard to various relevant elements.

Here is how both compare:

Leases and the Law

When it comes to leases and the law:

Residential property:

It is a shame that in multiple states across the US, residential property proprietors are not as protected as they should be. For instance, in the case of non-paying or problematic tenants, you will have to endure a lot of waiting before you can have them out of your property. It could take you as much as 9 months to evict them, which boggles the mind just thinking about it. Even if you are the proactive kind who is determined to throw out the problem tenant in the shortest time possible, it will still likely take you a minimum of 3 months before you can do so.

Commercial property:

Let us begin by taking note of this: commercial property leases can often be quite intimidating, and commercial property law may times too complex. However, unlike residential property investment, here, contractual law binds the leases. This means the lease will be whatever you and your tenant have agreed upon. It also means the lease is enforceable. It gets even better: you can stipulate absolutely anything in the lease and can expect the stipulations to be binding on both you and your tenant.

While we have pointed out that commercial leases can be complex beasts, the truth is that they can also be simple and one thing all commercial leases tend to have in common is the fact that they actually protect the property owner. Commercial leases do not renew automatically: you have the opportunity to renegotiate and there will be no rental caps imposed on you as long as you do not completely disregard the market. Oh, and dealing with non-paying tenants is easy: so long as they break the stipulations as dictated in the lease, you can throw them out ASAP without fear of backlash from the law.

Ease of Entry & the Financing Phenomenon

Here:

Residential property:

As it stands, putting 20% down is the requirement. We have in place loan programs that will allow you to put down significantly less than 20%, but you will have to pay higher interest rates and a bevy of other fees.

Financing rental property investment has always been easy; today, however, it is only relatively so because, for instance, the CMHC has seen it fit to consider only 50% of the income from your rental properties when calculating your income, which makes things a little more complicated when you have multiple properties.

Commercial property:

Financing commercial properties are usually the biggest factor when it comes to investing here. You are not required to put down 20%; down payments are 30% to 35%. Moreover, unlike that of residential property, CMHC never approves commercial investment financing. This means all your finances have to be in great order: you need to have excellent credit and you need to be willing to put some personal guarantees on your building of choice. Mortgage rates are higher as well.

As a beginner, it will be best if you start with little industrial/office/retail condos—there are tons of these on the market. Another starter option is to purchase a mixed-use property that has apartments on the upper floors and retail below.

The Familiarity Issue

Here:

Residential property:

Most people are familiar with this kind of real estate. It will be incredibly rare to come across somebody who has never rented an apartment or lived in a house. Most people are well acquainted with the structures and processes involved in the rental business: electrical issues, plumbing, air conditioning, and furnace fitting are not novel subjects, and with rental property, you will know much of what you need even if you have never invested in one before.

Commercial property:

Obviously, the level of familiarity will lean on the kind of property you purchase, but it is very likely that you will not be familiar with many building elements.

Take the example of checking out an industrial property that specializes in commercial laundry and is full of commercial laundry machines. Here, you will find machines and appliances you may have never seen before. You will have no idea of how badly they affect the electrical bill or if they will be culprits of noise pollution—of course, we are assuming you intend to take over the commercial property without changing a thing and allowing the existing businesses to run as smoothly as they have been up to that point.)

Risk of Vacancy

When it comes to this:

Residential property:

In truth, we need to say very little about this. Vacancy has been low for years now and this is perhaps residential property's greatest benefit over the commercial property. A residential apartment is unlikely to stay empty for too long.

Commercial property:

This is the trickiest part of commercial property investing. Commercial tenants can be hard to attract. It is also extremely important to evaluate the feasibility of the business housed in the property at that location. If you are renting out a pizza store, complete with pizzeria equipment, on a serene one-way street, you will likely never attract commercial tenants.

With this said, once you attract commercial tenants to your property, you are almost guaranteed to have them stay for years which differs from rental property where the traffic is a lot more active.

Investing In Commercial Property: The Objectives to Work Toward

Given that you are reading this book, you have your own batch of reasons for wanting to invest in commercial property. Perhaps you are a newbie real estate investor who has decided to do things the unconventional way by starting your investing ventures in commercial property. Perhaps you have already spent years in the property investment game and believe the time is ripe to move into commercial property investment. Perhaps you want the extra profits you believe will come with investing in commercial property. Whatever your reasons are, they are valid.

However, as far as investing in commercial property goes, if your vision is not clear, it will benefit you greatly to pause and consider your objectives. This section outlines material you can start with. By and by, you will be able to come up with definitive objectives for your investment.

Here are some objectives you may work toward by investing in commercial property:

1: You want to diversify your portfolio

Certainly, you cannot diversify your portfolio if you do not have one already. Thus, this objective is only suitable for those who have been active in real estate investment in some capacity.

With this said, it never hurts to grow and diversify your portfolio as a real estate investor. The more diversified your portfolio is, the better your credentials/reputation is. In addition to diversifying your portfolio, you may be looking to minimize investment risk by investing in a different type of property, which is a smart thing indeed.

2: Maximizing your income

This one is often the first objective on most peoples' lists. It would make little sense to invest in something if there was no chance of making a profit. If you are indeed trying to maximize returns, what sort of property are you looking to invest in at first? What is the rental return expected? Have you attempted to compare your figures with what similar properties are bringing in?

3: Growth of capital

If this is one of your objectives, you have to consider the subject of time. How much time do you plan to use up before you hit your preferred monetary figures and what are your figures anyway—how much do you intend to come up with?

4: Tax benefits

In real estate, Tax breaks and benefits are real and considerable. Here is a resource that covers this subject in depth:

https://www.biggerpockets.com/renewsblog/2015/05/20/tax-benefits-real-estate-investing-rental-properties/

With all we've discussed in mind, next, we will discuss the factors that determine property prices.

Factors That Influence Commercial Property Demand

This section will take you through the factors that have the most significant influence on commercial property demand. Usually, the closer you play by these factors, the easier you will be able to attract commercial tenants.

The reason why some commercial properties seem to have a steady stream of tenants in them while others, no matter how impressive the size and space, go for months without occupants, is because one party paid heed to the factors within this section while the other showed them little regard.

Factor 1: The Location

This is by far the simplest factor to understand. If you invest in commercial property in nowhere, Kansas, proceed to kit it out so that it resembles the inside of a spaceship and then place an advert calling for tech enthusiasts to rent your space, you will have a difficult time attracting any quality tenants.

Location, especially where commercial property is concerned, is everything. If your aim is to rent out your commercial property to a sub-section of tech gurus such as software developers, for example, the most important thing is to ensure your property is in a city or state where that sort of thing has a lot of traction. Otherwise, if you have to have your property in a place like Kansas, at least understand what they mostly do for business and then tune your property so that it caters to that.

Factor 2: Highest & Best Use

By highest and best use, we mean the present use of commercial property is not always the best use.

To elaborate this further, let me use a "Pizza store in a quiet one-way street" example; imagine you have made up your mind to invest in such a property. You walk into the space and immediately realize that the idea of a pizza store in such a place is not an ideal option because it is a bit hard to attract meaningful buyer traffic.

You could persist with the pizza store idea, in which case, you will likely have a difficult time attracting any pizza store people with any business sense. On the other hand, you could clean up the soot-stained walls, have all the grease cleaned off the surfaces, and transform the place so that it is suitable for business that thrives in that area. This way, you will have an easier time bringing tenants in. Once you invest in commercial property, make sure to determine if its current/previous use is indeed its best use. After doing this, make the necessary changes if any.

Factor 3: Cyclical Demand

They say that the man (or woman) who best adapts to changing times stands the highest chance of survival. This is very true in the commercial property world. Look at it this way. Residential property does not have many variations after all; besides maybe changing the position of the bed and replacing the wallpaper, what changes can you make to how you live? Commercial properties are different in that they allow for any number of variations.

Depending on how the economy looks, retail spaces may be in vogue for a spell of time. Other times, tech-office spaces, as well industrial and residential spaces (yes, residential commercial spaces—these days, the millennial generation likes to work, eat, play and live in the same space) will be all the rage.

You do not have to yo-yo all the time, tweaking your space to mirror the current economy swing. However, if the business is especially slow, consider doing it. You may be amazed at just how effective it can be.

Factor 4: Market-Driven Value

This alludes to the buyer or tenant's best offer versus that of the seller or property owner. To elaborate, this is not so much of a factor in the case of residential rental property primarily because a residential property owner can tweak rental/sale figures depending on how he likes them.

As we said earlier, commercial properties have their value determined by property valuation bodies. This means that as a commercial property owner, you do not really have 100% power valuation. Thus, depending on how the economic markets swing, you will likely have discrepancies in how you value your property—or what your rental figures are—with how the prospective tenants or buyers do.

There are times when the market-driven value will be superb and there will be an influx of commercial tenants or prospective buyers. Other times, however, this will not be the case and you may have a lean period.

Because property valuation bodies do not own you or your property, keep your finger on the economic pulse. When the market-driven value is especially low, consider lowering rental prices a little to match the market. A small tweak in pricing can be the difference between having a consistent stream of tenants and long, lean spells without tenants or buyers.

Factor 5: Shifting Demographics

This is one of the most powerful factors affecting not just the commercial property niche, but also the real estate markets as a whole. Here is something you should know—if you do not already know it: millennial fellows (millennial being a blanket term to describe the young/youngish group of people) are absolutely invading the workforce.

The bulk of them have very little interest in being in the employ of old-style companies and then taking 33 years to get to the top of the corporate ladder. Most of them are getting into the workforce as "expats" who run their own startups and are intent on making a financial killing in as quick and unhindered manner as possible. What can you do about this?

Well, if the intent is to change this dynamic, give up right now because what you can do about the dynamic is, you

21

guessed it, very little. However, as a commercial property investor looking to make a buck, you can do a million things.

You can style your spaces so that they are as attractive to this demographic as possible. You can pick properties to invest in that reflect the rental rates this group of people can afford. You can ensure the internet connectivity is as fast as possible or perhaps fit out the place with throw rugs and floor pillows. The number of things you can do to make your space attracting to millennials run into the millions.

As you get started, it is important to understand that while commercial real estate investing has its many benefits, it does come with some risks. Let's discuss that next.

The Risks of Investing In Commercial Property

Wise businesspeople are in the habit of saying that if someone is going to invest in something, it makes all the sense in the world to investigate the risks involved first and then evaluate his or her investment of choice and see if the positive feelings remain. This is valuable advice for you.

Commercial properties are very different to residential properties; you already know this. With commercial properties, you do stand to pocket higher returns, but quite often, investing in them presents a high risk-high reward scenario.

Risk factor 1: Economic shifts Influence Commercial properties more than any other property kind

In truth, economic shifts, especially if they are significant, will have an impact on all kinds of real estate. However, the biggest impact tends to be on commercial properties.

Take the example of a slow economy. The natural result of this is a high rate of unemployment. A high rate of unemployment will mean that the public is less eager to spend, which leads to lower spending levels. Discretionary spending ceases to become a thing for some people.

The very first industry to take a hit is the retail sector. In case this seems casual enough, consider that retail spaces are firmly in the commercial property category. The restaurants and pubs are second to feel the economic burn

(and you guessed it, restaurants and pub spaces are members of the commercial property sector.)

Can you see a pattern here? The transport, distribution, and manufacturing sector eventually become part of the list of the maimed. The cumulative result sees the value of retail spaces, office spaces, factories, and warehouses drop significantly as the vacancy rates start to rocket upwards. All this happens because the economy is bad, which has led people to stop spending nearly enough to keep the business world vibrant.

Compare this to the residential property market. No matter how badly people want to keep their keep, at the end of the day, they have to sleep somewhere, which means this particular market is not quite as affected.

Risk factor 2: Area fundamentals may change for the worse

When you are on the lookout for commercial property to invest in, you will want to make sure the place is easy to access and well placed when it comes to transport links. You will also want to make sure that the place is close to other businesses that will, in turn, support the businesses your tenants set up. You will want to keep an eye on how location holds up, which is a smart thing, all factors staying constant.

Herein lies the problem. Sometimes factors do not stay constant. What appears to be prime commercial real estate today may well prove to have been a massive waste of investment capital tomorrow. After investing, you may find out that the city council intends to knock down 90% of the buildings in the area—since they are too old—to make way for the construction of new ones.

Thus, no matter how to pinpoint your scouting was, you will find your good work foiled by matters you cannot control. The point is this. If you are going to invest in some property, make an effort to find out what the city council is planning to do with the area in the next 5 to 10 years. This should be easy enough to do. This brings us to...

Risk Factor 3: Zoning changes

This relates to the previously covered risk factor. It is a real possibility that zoning for the area your commercial property sits on could change from commercial to residential, perhaps because of newly formed suburbs proposed in the area. What can you do when the city council decides this is the way to go?

Unless your commercial property is one you can easily convert to meet residential use qualities, you may have to sell, prematurely so, your property to a developer for a lower price than you would like, or dig into your pockets and spend heavily on refurbishing the office space so that it meets the standards of a residential space. Both of these choices are not ideal for you in any way or form: you are neither looking to take a loss by being forced to sell your property nor looking to get into residential property via the expensive route of commercial real estate.

Again, before investing, make sure you understand what the city council has in mind for the area.

Risk factor 4: The oversupply phenomenon

This is rare but still a risk factor. You could invest in commercial property only to discover that the property is an area that has numerous other commercial spaces for rent. The result is usually fearsome competition that may force you to bend over backward—as they say—to be able to provide competitive rental rates, an unsavory situation to be in indeed.

Risk factor 5: The presence of upcoming infrastructure projects

Hold on for a second. Is this not a good thing? Is not the development of retail centers, motorways and train lines a good thing for you as a commercial investor? Surely, these things have a significant impact on people traffic, right?

Well, these things are indeed good things. Such projects are great... but only if they are happening in your area. If the infrastructure projects are happening away from your area, the effect may be very negative for you, with potential tenants drawn to the areas that are experiencing development.

Now that you understand the possible risks of investing in commercial real estate, now is time to finance your project. Let's discuss how to go about it next.

Financing Your Commercial Property Investment

As a newbie, and considering that investing in commercial properties tends to be more expensive than investing in residential properties, you may not have the capital necessary to make a cash buy and call it a day. If that is the case, you should not pull your hair out; loans can help you out.

However, the conventional loan you sign up for to help you invest in residential property will not do for commercial property. Commercial real estate loans differ from residential real estate loans.

This section will help you understand what to expect as well as the various types of commercial real estate loans available to you:

Understanding the Requirements for Commercial Property-Specific Loans

What are commercial investment property loans?

Your local bank will tell you that a commercial investment property loan is a loan designed either for a property with 5 units or more or for any non-residential investment property.

What can you expect from these loans?

You can expect 2 things from these types of loans:

1. Higher rates than would be the case with a residential investment property loan.

2. A shorter time length—as far as paying back the loan goes—with balloon payments due after five to seven years.

How do they differ from residential loans?

Commercial loans will differ from residential loans in a number of ways. They will look at similar standards as residential property investment loans but they tend to do this from a different angle. To understand this better, look at the points below:

Point 1: Debt to income

Regardless of what type of loan you are pursuing, a lender is always going to look at your debt and income. This is because debt and income are by far the metrics that will give the lender the most direct idea as to the kind of borrower you are.

There comes a time, however—such as when you are pursuing a multi-million dollar loan—when your personal income ceases to become very important to the lender. This is because, to be honest, if things hit a snag and your investment takes a turn for the disastrous, your job income is not going to foot the loan payment anyway.

For this reason, a lender will tend to examine your commercial property investment via a different lens. More than weighing your debt to income, the lender will base the decision on whether it makes sense to give you a loan on 2 vital questions:

1. Will your commercial property be able to provide any cash flow?

2. How much experience do you have when it comes to management? Do you show any qualities that convince of your ability to manage the business you want to set up? Before the thought of this sends you into a panic, to be eligible for a loan, the lender does not require you to be a CEO or to be in a management position. Simple things such as how your credit score is holding up and how you are handling outstanding loan payments will tell the lender a broad story.

With this in mind, what can you do to ensure you get a good loan deal?

1. Because it is harder to get a commercial property investment loan, be patient. It makes little monetary sense to jump at the first deal that comes your way. Take some time to think over the deal and seek to see if you can get a better deal. Move from one lender to the next and ask what loan deals they have to offer. The better the deal, the less you will suffer in a financial capacity—interest rates and the respective amounts tend to add up and if you are quick on the trigger, you may end up paying far more than you should.

2. When looking for a loan deal, portray and express yourself as a business owner—as opposed to a hobbyist—

at all times. This should be the case whether you are presently a business owner or not. It is important that the lender believes that he or she is not loaning money to an amateur regardless of whether you are actually one. One of the best ways to portray the image of a business owner is to...

3. Have a business plan in place. It does not have to be a fancy thing with 500 bulleted points. A simple but concise business plan with several key points carefully highlighted will be enough. A business plan convinces the lender that you have business ambition and the necessary organization and vision to make your ambitions a reality.

4. Know the answers to questions the lender may ask beforehand. It is unlikely that you have a crystal ball that will help you know the lender's questions beforehand. That being the case, it is not too hard to guess a few questions your lender may ask you. To determine if there is bound to be cash flow from your investment, for instance, your lender may ask you to explain what you plan to do with your property and what your 2/3/4/5 year plan is.

5. Think of your loan request as you would a job interview and ensure you arrive prepared.

Point 2: The credit score

Your credit score will still be a very important metric that the lender will use to judge your creditworthiness. Your credit score will show your ability to handle money and credit. Rates tend to differ from lender to lender but typically, a lender will expect you to have a minimum credit score of 720 or to walk.

Point 3: Loan to value

This one is much more relevant to commercial property investment loans than it is in residential property loans. A commercial lender will be a lot more cautious in ensuring that they are not being over-leveraged and that they have considerable equity in the deal.

What will the lender want? Usually, they will insist on a loan to value percentage of no less than 70% on the deal so that they are privy to 30% equity in the event that they need to foreclose and sell the property.

Point 4: Debt service coverage ratio

Also called the DSCR, the lender uses this ratio to evaluate a property's ability to generate income. The DSCR will compare the total income coming in (not inclusive of the mortgage payment you are making) with payment made on all debts. The equation looks like this:

DSCR = Net Operating Income / Debt Service

For instance, if the property's income sits at $10,000 a year and the yearly debt payment also sits at $10,000, your DSCR will be 1. A commercial lender wants a DSCR that is at least 1.2, which is to mean that after every expense is covered, there will be at least a 20% profit to keep things interesting.

Types of Commercial Loans for You

The following loan facilities are available for you:

Loan type 1: Bridge loans

A bridge loan will typically give you instant money to finance your project's immediate needs. They are, however, temporary loans that often have a term of about a year. A bridge loan is usually a loan obtained by the borrower in anticipation that he or she will receive a more substantial loan in the future.

A bridge loan, thus, will help set the stage for the main loan —it also sets the ball rolling so that it becomes even easier to get a long-term loan. To qualify for a bridge loan, you must possess excellent credit as well as show proof that you have enough cash to cover the existing expenses of the property as well as the loan amount.

Loan type 2: Real estate purchase loans

Here is a resource that covers this in some depth:

https://www.thebalance.com/types-of-commercial-loans-2866549

These loans are similar to both fixed and adjustable rate loans as far as salient properties go. You must have excellent credit, as was the case with bridge loans and, more importantly, have considerable savings in your bank and business accounts.

Loan type 3: Hard money loans

To qualify for a hard money loan, you have to list the commercial property you want to buy as collateral. Unfortunately, these loans are primarily offered by private lenders who cannot meet or are uninterested in meeting the stringent requirements in place for more mainstream lenders.

The result is a high risk of default and interest rates that can be absurd. Remember that you have to list the property as collateral; this will mean that should things go south, you are liable to lose any money you may have paid toward the loan as well as the property itself.

It looks unfair and likes the sort of court fodder that the jury likes to lap up, but nobody forced you to take these loans, which makes it harder for any court to rule in your favor. Here is a link that will take you to deeper coverage on hard money loans:

https://www.investopedia.com/articles/wealth-management/040216/using-hard-money-loans-real-estate-investments.asp

Loan type 4: Joint venture loans

A joint venture loan will be appropriate when you cannot raise enough capital or get an all-comprehensive loan deal on your own, and the same is the case with another party. You can join up, with the agreement to share profits fairly.

You can make the relationship with your partner official or not, or choose to extend it beyond or limit it to the financed property—the lender does not care and neither is he obligated to.

Having understood everything to do with finances, let's now get started with the first commercial property investment.

Your First Commercial Property Investment: How to Go About It

Taking the first step is always the most daunting part especially when it comes buying or investing in something. Regardless of whether you are investing in your first commercial property or buying your first brood of piglets, the first time is always the scariest primarily because you are on the unfamiliar ground and as such, are more wary of getting blindsided or making mistakes you did not know even existed.

Here are several steps you can follow to maximize the probability of success with your first commercial property. A lot of the steps and pointers here mostly call you to apply common sense and pick up as much knowledge as you can.

Step 1: Ask questions before making any moves

It makes little sense to move into new territory without assessing your situation and understanding what you are looking for. Here are some questions you will need to ask yourself first:

1. What sort of property am I looking for? Do I want to own office space, retail space, a restaurant/pub space, or is a nondescript car wash space more in line with my tastes?

2. What am I looking to do with my property? Am I looking to rent it out, hold onto it and enjoy subsequent tax breaks, or build equity?

3. Do I need to purchase the property outright or would a lease work?

4. What is my financing situation? Can I make the higher down payment that comes with a commercial property?

5. Am I willing to collaborate with another party? This is a great question to ask especially if you are thin on cash.

6. What is my risk tolerance?

7. How much time will I be able to dedicate to the property in a week once I invest in it?

8. Am I willing to perform property owner duties or will I sub-contract a service to carry out maintenance and pick up the rent?

Step 2: Visit and look at multiple properties

It is important that you visit as many properties as possible. Nothing beats being on site. You could receive a glowing account of some property from somebody else only to realize it is not quite as hot as the person described it. Likewise, you could get underwhelming accounts of a property only to realize the property is an absolute gem that only needs a personal touch and kitting out.

Of course, regardless of whatever else you are looking for, ensure that the pricing makes sense, the conditions are reasonable, and that the property location is great. This book has previously stated that location is an extremely important player: property that is in close proximity to hospitals, universities, and downtown areas will usually have high value and will rent out quicker.

Step 3: Look for, and find the experts you will need

As a newbie, you will need some experts to help you out with the oft-complex buying process. The kind of experts required, as well as the requisite number, will rely on the sort of property you are going for.

At the very least, you will need to hire a lawyer, accountant, a representative (think someone along the lines of a realtor), and a mortgage broker. If the property you want to purchase comes with more complexities than you bargained for, you may need to double down and look for more specialists such as accountants, tax experts, appraisers, notaries, and even environmental specialists.

In truth, there will be a lot of things you can cover on your own, given that you are not too shy of doing a little research and asking a few hard questions, but you may need to hire an expert on many other things as well.

Step 4: Figure out the state of your finances

The previous section takes you through the concept of commercial real estate loans as well as what you will need to stand a chance of getting a loan.

The next step is to figure out whom to approach for your loan. What banks, home mortgage companies, or credit unions make the most sense to you? Is your local bank a viable option or do their proposed interest rates seem a bit on the silly side? What is your credit score and is it at a place that makes it easier for lenders to consider loaning out to you? What can you do to improve your credit score—if it is in a dire state—so that you become more eligible for a loan? Would the present property owner consider assisting with financing—this is often rare primarily because the property owner does not know you and is more interested in making a buck above everything else; it does happen at times?

Step 5: Make your offer

For a novice, the smartest way to go about this is to do it via a real estate representative or realtor. Make no mistake, the seller will show up with his or her own rep or broker and will set the fellow loose on you if you are an inexperienced buyer acting on your own.

It is also smart to go through your lawyer as well. He or she will give you a letter of intent (LOI) that you will need to sign. This letter highlights the basic elements of the transaction. You could download a copy of an LOI from the internet. However, it helps not to be so cheap that you try to bypass the lawyer service—a lawyer will ensure the LOI is not binding in any way so that if you discover flaws in the property before completion of the purchase process, nothing shall bind you to an undesirable property.

Step 6: Due diligence & escrow

This is the stage where everything gets deathly serious. You are not prospecting anymore: money is about to swap hands. As such, you need to know as much as you can about the property you are looking to buy.

You will need an ALTA (American Land Title Association) survey conducted. This survey will provide vital info such as exact location of the main building and boundary lines. It will assist in the process of identifying easements (this includes access rights by various service corporations such as gas, water, rail, telephone, and other utilities.)

Then, both you and the seller need to find an escrow officer to act as a neutral 3rd party who oversees the transaction. This party will assist with the transfer of funds and deeds and will ensure your protection from unearthing rude shocks long after you have already paid up.

Oh, and you will have to pay for all of these. You will not be paying too much, but you will be paying nonetheless. However, consider this as insurance since paying will ensure you are getting value for money.

Next, we will be discussing some tips that will make your investment a success.

Vital Commercial Real Estate Investment Tips

More than ensuring you make a good start, the tips and strategies contained here will allow you to thrive in what is often a banana-skin type of investment for most people. Many investors, including seasoned ones, cannot wrap their heads around some basic commercial property elements—a great example is the need to move with the times and change up the property to fit the changing economy and markets.

Some market shifts heavily popularize retail spaces at the expense of other commercial property types. If you are flexible enough to package your space accordingly, you stand to profit from such. Many investors will either not understand some of these things or they will be too rigid to consider making a change.

Here are tips and strategies that will serve you well for a very long time:

Tip 1: Do not be an accumulator of properties; be an investor

The point of investing in something is to be able to turn a profit. Accumulating properties that bring very little by way of income is pointless. Sure enough, Tiny Rowland used to do this and he had quite some success. However, his gung-ho accumulation of properties and assets are perhaps the reason his legacy is not quite as great as it would have otherwise been.

Before investing in any property, take your time and make sure you pick winners regardless of how long it takes to find them. It is better to own a modest property that turns up profits than to own 10 properties that leave you feeling unsure of what to expect once end month comes.

Tip 2: Every commercial property has a lifetime

With time, you will have to revise the state of your property. The roof will need repairs, as will the walls, wallpaper, carpeting, floors, etc. Ensure you have a long-term plan so that your property is always in a competitive state.

Also true is that at times, retail spaces will be more popular. It makes sense to make changes when necessary. If a time comes when you are having difficulty renting out your retail space perhaps because of an economical shift, try kitting it out to become an office space or some other commercial space that is in vogue.

Tip 3: Focus on one type of investment at a time

This tip is here to serve a beginner. A time will come when it will be all right to combine as many commercial property types as you like since, at that future point, you will know most of what there is to know about various property types.

Nevertheless, right now, give your undivided attention to one investment type at a time. Focus on offices at first—if that is your preferred starting point—and only move on to the likes of retail once you have a thorough understanding of

41

renting out and maintaining office spaces. As they say, it is better to be a master of one thing than be an average fellow at many things. You do not want properties that perform averagely.

Tip 4: Seek a mentor and focus more on his or her mistakes

The idea of having a mentor is to safeguard you against as many mistakes as possible in addition to following the most efficient routes possible. You will mess up at points; a mentor's examples will help you understand what to prepare for or avoid.

A mentor will help you make the best decisions moving forward primarily because he or she has been in positions you will find yourself in. This will maximize efficiency, which will help you save the resources of time and money. Even better, mentors will help you notice things you may have otherwise missed.

Another thing a mentor will provide is connecting you with relevant persons in the commercial real estate market, people who would have otherwise been impossible to reach.

How to go about looking for a mentor

For starters, look for somebody you 'click' with as far as personality goes. If you are a quiet, introverted sort, a mentor with some traits similar to your disposition will be a good fit. If you are the intense, workaholic type, look for a mentor with a reputation for working very hard.

Tip 5: Determine if you have sufficient protection for your assets

The statement, *"everyone will be out to get a piece of you once you start succeeding"* sounds corny and insecure until you begin succeeding and realize it is just a plain truth.

It is hard to say what happens, but you suddenly become a target for lawsuits even if you play by the book and follow all the rules. The best way to ensure sufficient protection for your assets is to ask as many relevant questions as possible and then evaluate your answers:

1. What is at stake if I were to get slapped with a lawsuit and actually lose?

2. Is my property even protected? If so, how is it protected?

3. Is your PERSONAL property—such as your home and cruiser bike—protected?

4. Have you had the foresight to keep your investments completely separate from each other so that a lawsuit aimed at one does not trigger wholesale asset crumbling?

Besides not asking these questions, the worst thing you can do is guessing the answers to them. Either you have protective structures in place or you do not, in which case you are a sitting duck for lawsuits. Understand that people will not think twice about taking what is rightfully yours. It is up to you to protect what is yours.

Let's now debunk some myths that surround the commercial real estate.

Commercial Property Investment: Examining and Debunking Myths

Here are the most prevalently occurring commercial real estate myths as well as logical examinations of how valid they are. Given that they are myths, it does not take a 148+ IQ to tell that a lot of them are nothing more than bosh spread around by people who are too lazy or too intimidated to invest in commercial property.

Myth 1: Its extremely expensive and you need millions to get in

Just about anyone with a pulse seems to spread this particular myth. They will say that commercial real estate investment is too expensive to make sense of in a business sense.

It is true that to invest in commercial real estate, you will require larger investment amounts. However, it is a lie that you will have to pawn your liver and your spleen to be able to afford it. Just as is the case with residential property, we have available lenders who will determine how much you can put up and help you finance the rest of it. If anything, many lenders will put up more favorable lending rates for commercial property than residential property because they understand that these sorts of purchases have a higher profit potential.

Myth 2: You do not need a survey

This absurd myth is one that a surprisingly high number of newbies tend to believe. For some reason, people think it

45

makes sense to skip the survey partly because the property is for commercial use as opposed to residential use.

This is a logic blind spot—and even this is a generous assessment seeing as this is just not logical in any way. A survey will help you understand the state of the building and if it is in a good or bad condition.

Myth 3: If a commercial property is on sale, something must be wrong with it

Many people assume that if a commercial property is on sale, it must have a major flaw. Otherwise, why would somebody sell of a property that largely just sits there and brings him/her higher rental returns than a residential property would?

Well, it could be that the property owner is relocating or that there is a need to sell off some property to stabilize cash flow problems. It could be that the property owner wants to diversify his or her portfolio and as things stand, commercial property investments take up too much room. There are endless reasons as to why a commercial property may be on sale.

Myth 4: Investing in commercial property is excessively risky

Those who spread this one are afraid of any amount of risk, not just too much risk. If this is their state of mind, then the investment world, in general, is just not for them. They are also flat-out wrong:

Very few investments will offer an excellent and unpredictable a return rate as commercial property. While the commercial property market is admittedly more complex than the residential property one, the returns will far outweigh any risks you take.

Lastly, we will focus on the questions that people ask frequently about commercial real estate investing.

Commercial Property Investment FAQ

Here are some commercial property related questions that many new owners have. It could be that some of the questions here are already nagging you or will rise up once you have gone ahead and invested in commercial property:

Question #1: I am purchasing multiple commercial unit developments that already have tenants. Is it possible to change the terms of their leases?

It is not possible to change the terms of any existing leases unilaterally. However, it is not against the law to try to negotiate changes with the pre-existing tenants. You may also know that tenants will be hard-pressed to accept lease term changes that do not favor them unless of course, you have several catches within your changes that offer them some other benefit in return.

Question 2: What additional costs can I expect when buying a commercial property?

You must budget for legal fees since legal evaluation is one buying aspect you do not want to skim over or overlook. In addition to legal fees, ensure you have money set aside for SDLT (Stamp Duty Land Tax) as well as Land Registry fees. You will also bring in some surveyors to help you know how the property is holding up; have some money set aside for them.

In many cases, the payments you make will prove far more valuable than you could have bargained for them to be. Take the example of bringing in a proper surveyor with experience in his or her field. Such a person will be able to advise you on several things you may have overlooked and given you price estimates of both repair and purchase costs that you will know to be accurate.

Question 3: Is VAT a fixture in commercial properties?

Commercial properties are not liable for VAT, which should come as good news. It gets even better though: as the VAT non-paying owner, no law prevents you from electing to charge VAT on supplies made with regard to your property with the inclusion of selling and renting. Whether you choose to charge VAT from your tenants is up to you.

Question 4: How difficult will it be to change the use of the commercial property?

There is no straightforward answer to this question. How hard it will be to change the use of a commercial property will depend on what the commercial property is presently used for and what you intend to change its use to. Needless to say, it will be easier to convert a retail space to an office space than it will be to change a pub space into the same.

Question 5: My tenant is selling his lease. Do I have a say in the kind of business he chooses to sell it to?

Most leases will oblige the tenant to obtain your consent before selling the lease. It is not feasibly possible to withhold consent unreasonably to a lease sale, but it is well within your rights to ask what the proposed use of the incoming tenant is as well as their covenant strength (what their ability to pay rent is, and how well they are suited to following the stipulations under the lease).

Most leases will not place limits on the type of use the property is put in, but if your tenant wants to sell his lease to a group of welders while all the spaces surrounding his are quiet, white-collar office spaces, you have every right to block such a move.

Conclusion

We have come to the end of the book. Thank you for reading and congratulations on reading until the end.

I truly hope that you found the book eye-opening on how to invest in commercial real estate even if you are a complete beginner.

If you follow the directives put forth by this beginner's manual to investing in commercial property, a misstep will be a rare occurrence. Still, it helps to broaden your knowledge as much as possible.

Use other resources to support the contents of this book and remember that when it comes to commercial properties, location is extremely important. You can get away with owning residential property several tens of miles from the commercial business center of your state, but as a commercial property owner, doing so is detrimental.

If you found the book valuable, can you recommend it to others? One way to do that is to post a review on Amazon.

Click here to leave a review for this book on Amazon!

Thank you and good luck!

www.ingramcontent.com/pod-product-compliance
Lightning Source LLC
Chambersburg PA
CBHW030035230526
45472CB00002B/530